How To Become A Golf Contender

by Rhandy X. Jedermann

Citizen of the USA, Resident of Earth, & Golf Enthusiast

Author Note

This book written in memory of my good friend Bernie

one of God's kindest creatures.

This copyrighted work of non-fiction was completed in January of 2019 and has been registered at the U.S. Copyright Office. The author retains all rights to printing, storing, or otherwise reproducing this material in any form whether it be by digital, photographic, or mechanical printing processes. The Bowker ISBN (International Standard Book Number) for this print publication is:

978-1-73269-802-4

Any reproduction of the contents of this work requires the author's permission in writing and such inquiries should be directed to

Rhandy X. Jedermann

NeutronDelux Publishing

P.O. Box 962

Sylvania, Ohio 43560

Most of the names contained here have been changed to protect the privacy of those individuals, but the facts of this story are delivered in manner that I hope will entertain as well as enhance your approach to and enjoyment of the game of golf and possibly the rest of your life as well.

Abstract

This book presents some methods and attitudes about the game of golf (and life) that are intended to help the non-athletes among us. My goal in writing this is to help the reader acquire the basic methodology needed to successfully compete under the golf handicap system and hopefully see their names one day on their local clubs winner of the year trophy.

Keywords: golf, contender, golf mechanics, competitive edge in golf, golf fundamentals, attitude, golf psychology, life's learning continuum, self help in golf, swing analysis.

TABLE OF CONTENTS

Introduction to Rhandy X. 'the Contender'

Chapter 1:	The Grip
Chapter 2:	Alignment & the Stance
Chapter 3:	Your Feet, Waggle, & Practice Swing
Chapter 4:	The Take Away & See You at the Top
Chapter 5:	The Down Swing & Follow-through
Chapter 6:	Equipment
Chapter 7:	Record Keeping, Swing Keys Card, Yardage Card, and measuring progress
Chapter8:	Putting is ……….Half the Game
Chapter9:	Physical Conditioning & Mental Preparedness
Chapter10:	The Game of Games, Honor of the Game, the Mystique of Golf

INTRODUCTION to Rhandy X. "the Contender"

For those of you who have read my first two books on gaming titled "Gaining Your Personal Edge @ Casino Bank of America" and "Sharpen Your Edge On Double-Zero Roulette", (both available at LuLu.com and Amazon, etc.) you already know my attitudes about gaming and life in general. These games we play reflect heavily on who we are as personalities.

I explained in those previous volumes, that I spent 35 years as a Product Development Chemist for one of the world's largest and most respected chemical companies and those patented inventions created a substantial flow of cash into that huge machine. Now in retirement, I get to use some of that same methodology to extend my gaming pursuits.

I know some of my acquaintances are apt to say, "I found your books on gambling a little surprising coming from someone like you". My response to that person would be that the methodology used for my roulette book is in fact very similar to many of the techniques used to do the investments in their own personal 401K stock portfolio.

To me it is interesting that all of us gamble in many different ways during our time on earth and most people are oblivious to most of that. In addition, we are even less aware of the methods employed to deliver those services. In this piece of literature, I will try to reveal some of the methods that I have found successful in my golfing hobby.

My other books were written to accomplish two purposes. The first to prove that the "game that can't be beaten" can actually be defeated with the proper methodology and discipline and secondly, I wanted to de-mystify the game of roulette that seems to have a legion of lemmings marching off the financial cliff every day in casinos all across the country.

This book on golf may seem more innocuous, but is in many ways similar to those books on gambling games. Golf is filled with many risk and reward situations and strategies to minimize hazards. Success at golf also relies heavily on the concept of 'hedging your bets'. The game of golf is almost always won by the player who is able to play within the limits of his own sometimes meager abilities. When we try too hard, we often defeat ourselves as our opponents appear to effortlessly cruise along to victory.

I am writing this book for an audience that is for me pretty self-descriptive. It is for those people who are not natural athletes in any physical sense of the words. I am aiming this book at those people who might describe themselves as fairly un-coordinated, but fascinated by the game of golf. The extent of my personal athletic trophies was getting my High School Letter based on my Chess team performance. For people like us, the hope for success in golf lies within the handicapping system and also the fact that the ball is not moving until we strike it!

This book presents an approach to golf that can probably be described as eclectic. For me it is the accumulation of about twenty-five years of trial and error and extensive reading on the subject. I will only present material to you, that has personally helped me in my pursuit of improvement in my golf game.

In some respects, my techniques for mastering golf are quite similar to that casino conquest I mentioned earlier. Why do most people never improve their performance?............wait for it................because they never document anything!!!!

I invite you now to join me in the passionate pursuit of the game of golf that should feel like personal success and personal enlightenment. 'The Game of Games' beckons us to give it our most sincere effort possible so that we too, can one day raise our local club's championship trophy. We will then know that our name deserves its' rightful place inscribed there along-side all those other previous champions.

Chapter 1: **The Grip**

I should probably not assume too much about you the reader as I tell this story. You probably have a general awareness of the game of golf as seen on television. Many of us lesser mortals play just for fun and camaraderie with our friends and relatives. We often play a slightly relaxed version of the game that many of us refer to as 'winter rules'. This common practice allows us to put a 'respectable' number on the scorecard even when we have had a horrendous series of misfortunes on one of the holes.

These winter rules most often include allowing us to roll the ball off hardpan compacted dirt onto a grassy turf so we have a reasonable chance of contacting the ball with the face of our club. At our club which has pretty substandard bunkers, we are also allowed to lift our ball and rake the compacted sand prior to hitting our sand shot. This is allowed so it doesn't feel like we are playing off a slab of concrete when we are in the sand trap. Whatever version of golf you play, make it a point that everyone in your group knows what version is being played prior to the start of play. This is a good way to be sure everyone knows that a casual, friendly round of golf is beginning.

This chapter is titled The Grip so let's see if we can 'get a grip' on the reality of this game. Why start here? If you think about the grip, it represents our only direct connection to influencing the ball's behavior and after all that is really at the heart of this game. We intend to make the ball cooperate with us in ways that at first may seem impossible and also counter-intuitive.

The term grip of course has multiple definitions. In golf we are concerned with both the physical rubber grip on the handle of our golf club as well as the manner that our hands hold the club during the golf swing. Both of these are 'grips'.

Let's talk first about the rubber grip on the club. I am amazed that so many amateurs play with grips that are old, slippery, and certainly are adding extra strokes to their scorecards. A new, high quality grip only costs about five bucks and you can easily install them yourself if you have a gripping vise in your garage. If you don't, your pro shop or golf retailer will often install a grip for a couple extra dollars.

My old friend Bernie had a bad habit of never replacing his old grips. One afternoon we stood on the 17th green of a local course. When Bernie hit his tee shot the driver flew out of his hands during his follow through and his club helicoptered about 30 feet up into the top of a nearby tree. A group of guys on the adjacent tee box started to laugh hysterically. Bernie glared in their direction for a couple of seconds, but he couldn't say much. We turned our attention back to his lost club as it made its' way down to the ground a few seconds later. He was lucky there was a slight wind helping him with the retrieval effort. Enough said about slippery grips. New, clean, and tacky wins the race in optimal grip condition.

As our only connection to striking the golf ball, our connection to the club is controlled by how we apply our hands to the club. Many players are very sloppy and inconsistent in their approach to golf and life in general. They probably do it differently each time and guess what. Their result is different (and unpredictable) each time too.

Arnold Palmer liked to tell the story of how his father taught him about the grip as a young boy. His father placed the young Arnold's hands on the club in their proper configuration and his father said "now keep them there". I have to agree with his Dad. Once you have learned a sound grip, it should last a life time. I will teach you the grip (for a right-handed golfer) used by one of the greatest women golfers of the modern era, but I actually learned my preferred grip method a couple of years prior from an article titled "The Grip by David Lee". At that time in 2011, it was available on www.reviewgolf.com and I will condense it down to the fundamental principle that makes it great.

Why do I use the word great? Because this grip technique solves a major problem that probably 50% of the amateurs out there suffer from. It effectively neutralizes the problem of gripping the club too tightly. When you do this a whole list of bad things result. The resulting tight arm muscles dramatically slow down swing speed, it promotes blocked shots (usually a line drive to the right), and it makes it difficult to do a full follow through.

The David Lee description of the left hand gripping the club is very similar to the way Ben Hogan describes the left-hand grip in his classic book "Five Lessons: The Modern Fundamentals of Golf" written by Ben Hogen in 1957 and a must for every golf fans book shelf. What David Lee adds that is really to me a significant improvement on Hogen's description, is the concept of tightly 'cinching' the club with the pinky and ring finger of the left hand.

This cinching concept allows the wrist and arm to remain free of excess tension and allows the arms to swing freely through impact. It also allows a full follow through which is in most cases desired. You know that you are using the David Lee grip properly, if you are able to hold the club out in front of you supported only by those last two fingers and the muscular pad at the heel of your left palm.

This sort of grip is very similar to the one promoted by another modern great in the game namely Annika Sorenstam. She uses a grip very similar to Hogen's grip, but calls hers "A Six Finger grip" referring to that muscular pad on her hand as her sixth finger.

We should remember that the golf swing is really a left hand driven activity and the right hand is really only along for the ride and some minor stabilization activity. If you don't believe me, imagine as a right hander having to choose one hand or the other to use to swing the golf club (not both). If we try to use only our right arm, it feels to me that it is very easy to "come over the top" and slice the ball severely to the right rough. This is the swing flaw that 80% of the high handicap golfers out there suffer from. If we try to swing the club with only our left arm, the result to me feels like my arm becomes a natural extension of the club and the club head approaches the ball from the proper inside pathway to the ball promoting straight ball flight or a slight draw to the left (more on these concepts of slice to the right and draw to the left later in the book).

As we add our right hand lightly to the grip, we can choose the classic interlocking grip or the baseball grip if that feels better to your personal physical makeup. In the interlocking grip, the pinky finger of your right hand slips in to interlock with the index finger of your left hand (which is already in place on the golf club). This configuration of a slightly stronger 'cinched' left hand and a slightly weaker stabilizing right hand works very well to deliver good control of the golf club especially at the top of your back swing where it is most likely to become mis-aligned.

Chapter 2:   Alignment & the Stance

Alignment really refers to the point that we are seeking our ball to go to. In seeking our destination and goal, proper alignment often becomes a problem for many golfers. The alignment challenge in golf is that we are essentially forced to stand off to one side of the target line as we play. For that reason, alignment behavior is quite different than in archery or darts where we are allowed to lock our eye on the target as we play.

In golf we lock our eye on the ball prior to swinging the club and therefore we need to develop some techniques that help to insure our alignment is fairly accurate. From the experimentation I have done, I would say if you create an alignment strategy that delivers the ball within a 10° arc on the fairway, then you have done well. When you are putting on the green, you should be able to create a technique that cuts that arc down to one or two degrees (more on that in Chapter 13).

There are two techniques that I have found over the years that work well to give me confidence that my alignment is reliable. Before I describe those techniques, I want to explain something that Sam Snead (one of the greatest golfers of all time) used to say about the golf swing. He was trying to convey the idea that all of us have slightly different bodies and physiology. Our joints have slight variations and limitations and therefore our swings all take on a slight uniqueness that also varies from day to day.

The fact that the condition of your spine and associated musculature varies continuously helps explain a lot about the inconsistency in our swings that we find so vexing. The way Sam Snead expressed the concept was "You have to dance with the one you brought". Meaning you have to accept this variability and adapt slightly to whatever your body is delivering to you on that particular day.

The first alignment technique that has been helpful for me is the realization that the best neutral alignment aid is the following. As I stand ready to strike the ball, I grip the shaft of the club with my left hand on the club's grip and the right hand holding the shaft of the club. Both hands are separated by a space of about 24 inches. With arms straight, press the shaft against the front of both thighs and see if the club shaft is pointing along the target line. If it does, you made a good guess. If the club shaft is not pointing at your target, you should pivot around until your right leg finds the place where the club shaft is pointing down the target line. Your body is now in good alignment to propel the ball down that target line.

I have found that if you then feel like you need a little more of a draw, you can pull your right foot back from the target line several inches and if you need more of a fade to the right (a gentle slice) you can advance your right foot several inches forward toward the target line. From there your body is now aligned and you are ready to proceed with addressing the ball.

The other alignment technique that works for me (especially with my driver) is to vary the distance at address from the club face to the back of the golf ball. This may not work for everyone, but for me it works very well. What I find is that by varying that distance from about 0.25 inch to about 1.25 inch behind the ball, I can direct ball flight to either right or left fairway. Close to ball goes right and far away goes left.

If I start with a gap of 0.75 inch behind the ball and my first drive is going toward the left rough, then I will start using a smaller 0.25 inch gap to bring it back to the center of the fairway. If my initial drive using 0.75 inch gap produces a push to the right, then I will increase the gap to bring the ball flight more to the left and hopefully the center of the fairway. I have a reputation for being a very good (in the fairway) driver of the golf ball and that is how I accomplish that accuracy. When you see the pros on television, just before the start of their round, where are they? On the range evaluating the kind of things that I just described. They are making minor adjustments.

Now that we are aligned, we should discuss how we stand there holding our golf club. First and foremost, our spine should be fully straight and not slouching. If we feel a slight tension or tightness in our lower back, it is probably as straight as needed. Your spine is the hinge that your golf swing rotates around as it travels on it trip into the backswing and then the return trip back to meet and swing through the golf ball.

The second key feature of the stance is the arms and where they are at address. The arms which are gripping the club should be hanging pretty much straight down and for me should be so close to my torso that my elbows lightly touch my ribcage.

I say touching the ribcage, because later during the takeaway, we should feel that the arms and torso are both turning initially at the same speed as we create stored energy in our resistance muscles. The arms that hang downward during the stance should in fact be fully extended so we have a good sense of what actual club face to ball impact will look like.

This point is actually very important. Centrifugal force which occurs during the swing of the club actually brings the combination of lower/upper arm to a fully extended state. (I've read a lot of golf books and don't believe I have heard that concept verbalized). For me those fully extended arms represent success and the difference between center of the clubface impact instead of hitting the ball very high on the clubface.

You are not quite ready to make a very respectable swing, but you are getting close. Before we are actually ready to swing into the ball, we need to understand the importance of our feet, the waggle, and the practice swing.

Chapter 3: Your Feet, Waggle, & Practice Swing

Feet are one of God's greatest creations and if we understand them, they can put some real power into our golf swing. Sam Snead used to like to practice barefoot and after my explanation I think you may understand why.

For those of you who have other athletic pursuits like softball, fly casting, or even frisbee you probably understand the dynamics of throwing a ball, swinging a baseball bat, casting a fishing lure, or throwing a frisbee. All these activities are very similar to a successful golf swing and all contain the concept of storing energy in spring-like tension and then a weight transfer from one side of the body to the other side as we deliver and use that stored energy.

For me this actually was a persistent problem for me during my early learning stages. I was able to transfer energy and weight into my backswing, but could not transfer it back to my left side. I was effectively "trapped in my back swing". It is very good advice to occasionally have someone photograph or take a short video of your golf swing. Examination quickly reveals 'things that are out of place'.

As I look at my personal swing photos, I see that I have completed a shot and my error is obvious. Instead of most of my weight ending on my left foot where it should be at the swing's completion, the photo shows that all my weight and energy is still stuck on my right side. Very little energy was then available to be delivered to my left side and the ball at impact.

For me the answer to this problem was very slow in coming and in fact most authors offered me no solution to this problem. Let me say that much of the turning point in my golf hobby came about by a very chance encounter at a garage sale. I bought an out of print book by Leslie King for $2 which changed everything for my game. King's book printed in 1976 and titled as "Master Key to Good Golf" was the first such book that fully explained to me the 'why' of the golf swing.

I decided to read the whole thing with the intention of taking the whole instructional package as the gospel truth and not cherry-pick bits and pieces to use in my hodge-podge of a game. Once I did this, the transformation was immediate. I went from being last place in my league to nearly winning the title a couple years later.

Once you read a book like this, you will realize how players like Jim Furyk, Bubba Watson, and John Daly can exist and reach the top of their game without the huge entourage of coaches and trainers that many of today's modern pros seem to require. In fact, it helps prove the point that perhaps one lifetime coach or maybe even none are required to reach the top of the game.

The real point I am trying to make is that lessons and coaching are great, but when you are on the course playing, you have to be the one making corrections to your game as the action progresses. To do that, you need to understand the inner-workings of 'your' swing and how to tweak whatever it is delivering on that particular day.

As for the role of the feet in the golf swing, my particular issue was not ironed out until I went to the practice range and proved the solution to myself. What disturbed me was that I had not seen the solution to my problem (in print) until much later. I found my answer when I happened to see Larry Nelson sharing his story on the Golf Channel. Larry has a body type very similar to my own and he said a couple of things that made my ears perk up. I looked up an interview he had done and there it was!

He claimed that in order to gain consistency in your swing, you need to stay in balance. For him that meant his weight was on 'the balls of his feet' as he set up and actually performed the full golf swing. Finally, I had received literary confirmation for the same answer that I had discovered myself at the range.

I had found that once my right heel got loaded up in my backswing, I would invariably get stuck there in my back swing and could not transfer my weight back to my left foot during the forward swing of the golf club. I proved that when I consciously shifted 60% of my weight onto the balls of my feet, I was able to make that weight transfer from left to right and back to the left again without any hesitation or delay.

Instead of being stuck in my back-swing, the weight and energy now smoothly transferred back to my left side and good things happened in the form of solid ball striking and good energy transfer to the ball. I can only say: "thank you Larry Nelson for sharing your story".

Now that we fully understand the roll that our feet play, lets figure out what a waggle is and how it helps us. In recent years, many of the pros have not been displaying much of a waggle before striking the ball, with the notable exception of Jordan Spieth. He generally places the club head behind the ball and does a false takeaway or waggle about three times behind the ball and then executes the shot trying to duplicate the path he had just traced out in his mind. This is something that will certainly help many of us high handicap amateurs and is worth trying in our pre-shot routines.

The other concept that is also beneficial to many players is the visualization and muscle-memory building that you get in doing a successful practice swing right before the real shot is executed. Let me just add one short story to reinforce this point properly.

Some years ago, while I was struggling on a Jack Nicklaus course in Mexico, my golfing buddy says right after I duffed a tee shot: "Rhandy, why don't you just use your practice swing? You've got a great practice swing!" He was right, most of us do have a great practice swing, but we always try to 'add a little something' to it as we deliver our real swing. Don't do that, use your practice swing. You will be pleasantly surprised.

Another concept closely related to the waggle is your body position at the point of impact of the clubface and the ball. When we passively set up to the ball and place our golf club behind the ball, our entire body is in a very symmetrical type of formation. What I mean is that both sides of our body are present at set-up as nearly mirror images of each other with the ball sitting near the middle line of that body symmetry. What we should realize and hold in our minds is an image of what our actual 'impact position' should look and feel like.

You can easily recreate the impact position you desire by doing a simple drill. Stand to the ball and do your full set-up. Now instead of striking the ball, set your body into slow motion and bring the club and your entire body into a swing sequence stopping the club face one inch from the ball and freeze. This approximates your real impact position.

If you are able to see yourself in a mirror now, you should see and feel your impact position. It's quite different from that passive position you assumed earlier. You now have 80% of your weight on your left side and the full symmetry of your body has disappeared. Your entire body has probably shifted about three or four inches to the left as you reached that stop-action freeze point.

Some amateurs can go through years of playing, without gaining any awareness of this point. We need to remember that the golf swing is a dynamic series of motions and not an archery competition where we just aim and pull the trigger. The above drill is a good one to add to your pre-shot routine and I would give it a lot of credit for helping many people hit the ball on the center of their club face instead of a less desirable impact point.

Chapter 4:   The Take Away & See You at the Top

The takeaway is where golf starts to become interesting. We now enter the phase of dynamic movement and also the contradictions of golf begin to show themselves. One of the beauties of this game is that many things are not quite as they first seem.

A person seeing the full golf swing for the first time might say, "well you just use your arms to raise the club up and then you use your arms to make the club come down to the backside of the ball". I would say that statement is really about 20% correct and here's why. The greatest amateur golfer of all time, Bobby Jones probably said it best when he said "I spent my career swinging a weight at the end of a string."

The golf swing we wish to emulate is really a combination of motions that should not be fully separated from each other. The golf swing is primarily a twisting and untwisting of our entire body and it is also the addition of the arms and club traveling along at the same time. We are not hammering a nail, where essentially the whole process is limited to the muscle group of a single arm. We are instead setting our entire body in motion in order to swing that weighted string.

If we don't attempt to turn our body into a coiled spring during the take-away, we end up with only our arms to supply the energy we need for ball striking. Unfortunately, most people's arms tend to be some of the smaller, less powerful muscles in their body and do not offer all the potential power needed to effectively propel our golf ball. The second problem with an arms-only swing is that we get into a scooping kind of geometry that does not use the shape of the club head to its' greatest efficiency.

To work well the golf swing must start with a turning of our torso away from the target and we will effectively 'turn our back' toward the ball's eventual target. As your torso starts its' turn, the arms and club must also begin rotating back at the same pace. We don't want the arms to get ahead of our torso and we also don't want the arms and club to lag behind either. The trick I use, is to think of and be aware of my right elbow lightly touching my rib cage as the club begins to go back. Actually, I begin that backswing with the torso and arms starting back simultaneously.

Of course, none of us are rubber-bands except maybe Johnny Miller during his very skinny heyday. As our bodies turn into our back swing, they reach a point of resistance when the muscles have attained their stored energy limit. In the classic golf swing the arms and club continue upward into the full 100% backswing position, where the club shaft is level with the ground and club head is pointing at the target. But, stop right there. Are you or I athletic enough to get the club up there? More importantly, from that position are we able to deliver it on the right swing path back down to the ball? Virtually all of us have to answer no.

The correct solution to this limitation in skill, balance, and flexibility is a concept taught by many teaching professionals. That concept is the idea of the three quarter (3/4 or 75%) backswing. For myself and many others, this concept is the difference between loving the game or deciding that the game is just too frustrating.

When your arms swing upward to that 75% backswing position, you will stop briefly and while still in balance, begin to deliver the club to the proper pathway back down to the ball.

In order to make this a smooth transition from backswing to downswing, I use the following technique. During the travel of the club from the address position up to that ¾ position, I silently say to myself "one, two, three, and swing!" What this does is allow the club to reach the top and be in a stable, properly aligned position, just prior to beginning a smooth approach downward to the ball. Remember, a quick jerky backswing never produces any good results.

Reaching the top of your backswing is a very important point in the swing. Now that you have reached the top of your ¾ backswing, what should you be thinking or more importantly feeling at this point? Here is what I have found. When it feels right, you have done the things needed to get there correctly.

If you have arrived there correctly, you should feel the resistance of your right leg and foot preventing any further turning action by your body. These loaded-up large muscles signal the completion of the backswing energy storage. At the same time, you should feel the ball of your left foot pressing the ground firmly and also limiting further coiling of your body even as your left heel lifts slightly off the ground. The combined tension of both legs might make you think of a scissors like action to prevent you from falling off a horse.

You should also feel at the top of your backswing a distinct tightness in the muscles below your left shoulder that extend down the left side of your chest. This is another indication that these muscles have fully loaded themselves with potential energy to use very soon during the downswing.

Also, at the top of that ¾ backswing, the left arm remains very close to straight and the elbow does not become another moving part (for amateurs, that bent left elbow only increases the odds that we won't be able to fully return to a proper impact position).

As we stand poised for a split second at the top, our eyes should stay locked on the golf ball. By doing this we gain a keen sense of awareness of where everything is in relation to the ball. We know where our hands are, we know where the club head is, we know where our spine is, we know where both shoulders are, and also where our pelvis is as we begin the downswing.

How do we start that downswing? Not with any violent jerking downward with the hands cradling our club. I believe the best way to start down is to use that "one, two, three….." technique described earlier along with an easing of the tension in the left knee and slight bump toward the target with that left knee. At the same time the left arm and the back of the left hand is allowed to chase down the target line toward the target.

Ah, but you ask "what about the ball?" Let's just say the ball happens to get in the way of our swinging club. In fact, let's say the ball is precisely in the pathway of the center of our club's face and the ball streaks in a powerful trajectory down the center of the fairway in near perfection.

In the next chapter we will talk more about the downswing and impact position.

Chapter 5: The Down Swing & Follow-through

As we contemplate dropping the club down from the top of our backswing, we should think of that waggle activity we did during our pre-shot routine. That waggle made a groove in our muscle memory and also our subconscious about our proper pathway to the ball. If we have had our eyes locked on the ball, we should have enough trust generated from prior practice to know that we will make good contact with the ball as we swing along that target line.

We might be tempted to only think about striking the ball, but we should think instead about swinging the club through the place where the ball is sitting. This sort of thinking promotes a full swing through the ball, that does not give up at the point of impact. That full swing fully delivers all that right-side stored energy and weight and brings it back fully to the left side in a golfer balanced on his left foot and barely any weigh remaining on that right foot.

At that conclusion of the swing, your belt buckle as well as the front of your shirt are both facing the target. The club and your hands have traveled around your body and the club head and shaft (now above your left shoulder) are pointing fully away from your target.

Congratulations to you, on the initial mental completion of a successful swing of the golf club and the accompanied flight of the ball that happened to be in the way.

Before going on to the next chapter, I want to share the most significant golf concept that I have seen in my last thirty years of reading books and magazine articles. This article relates to the concept of the swing plane that your club follows in order to effectively find the golf ball during your downswing. This concept had been a personal torment for me until the early months of 2011.

At that time of winter, I was going to my local indoor golf range and trying to fully master the driver (for most players the hardest club to master). I had struggled with trying to make my swing look like the professional swings that I had seen on television just about every weekend. My results using this 'attempt-to-mimic' concept were not pretty and were in fact very frustrating.

I thought, "I am going to experiment and see if I can make this work". I began to do a variety of different setups and angle approaches before the actual swing and guess what happened. I found one approach that actually began to yield effective and repeatable results! The ball was going on a powerful and straight pathway and I suddenly felt confident and in control of my game!

You should be asking "what exactly did you do?". What I did is exactly what was shown one year later (Feb. 2012) in Golf magazine in an article titled "<u>Find Your Perfect Swing</u>" by Top 100 Teacher Mike Adams. I rank this article as number one in importance for the golf game of Rhandy X. What I had proven that night in the indoor range in 2011 was that I was a Low-Track golfer. This means that due to the physiology of my arms (which are 1" shorter than the average) I should swing the club on a very flat plane for best results.

You too, need to determine whether you are a Low-Track, Mid-Track, or High-Track golfer. This knowledge to me is the Holy Grail of the golf swing. Read the article and find out from Mike Adams who you really are as a golfer.

In the next chapter we discuss equipment and how that relates to our bid to become contenders.

Chapter 6:   Equipment

In this chapter we come to the equipment involved in this wonderful hobby. So far, we have been swinging our imaginary clubs at our imaginary golf ball. Now let's get back to the reality of our physical plane and down to earth. For me, my personal equipment has taken on many yearly refinements to better suit my increasing abilities.

My golf equipment is good and fits my particular game well, but I do not have a fortune tied up in this part of my hobby. Let's talk first about the irons in your bag. These are the clubs that might be described as the middle of the set. They are not the drivers or fairway woods or hybrids. These middle irons are usually viewed as probably the 4-iron through 9-iron and for most amateurs they propel the ball between about 100 and 170 yards.

These mid-irons are usually the second club we employ as we follow a successful tee shot with our driver or our 3-wood. Often when we are holding these middle irons, we are standing far down the fairway focused on delivering the ball into the surface of the green. If we are really playing well and have become a good driver of the golf ball, we will be using the shortest most accurate iron in this group which would be our 9-iron. As we go along in our golf journey, we will have notations written down that tell us what our typical yardage is for each club in our bag. More about that later in Chapter 7.

If we were only allowed to practice with one club from each group discussed, I would say make yourself familiar with the feel of the 6-iron. For many years, club companies would come out with new equipment lines and the demo clubs were always 6-irons. As my personal sets have evolved over the years, I would always take the new and old 6-irons to the back yard and do a rigorous comparison with a wiffleball. These perforated practice balls never break a neighbor's window and always deliver good relative feedback when you compare two clubs. Take out an odd number of wiffleballs like five or seven and start aiming for a target in the yard.

What you will learn will probably surprise you. You will discover that your old club hits that group of seven wiffleballs an average of say 25 yards and the width of the dispersion pattern is maybe 13 feet wide. Then you do the same thing with your new club and your average distance for seven wiffleballs is now 27 yards and the width of dispersion is tightened down to 10 feet wide.

I have done these wiffleball evaluations over the years with all my clubs except the putter of course. The results have always revealed the difference or equal kind of performance for the new equipment. This method comes very close to predicting what you will see as you hit a real golf ball at the range or on the course. If you have a backyard area 80 feet long, these wiffleballs can offer you a great way to practice that translates very well to actual play when you arrive at your course.

The next group of clubs to consider are the driver and fairway clubs. The driver, although it is the largest and longest of your clubs is in fact the lightest club that you will swing. Choose one that is forgiving and try it out (if possible) before you buy. I generally buy a good quality driver on e-bay when it is about a two-year-old model. This brings those high prices down dramatically and I have never been burned after purchasing about 30 clubs on e-bay over the years.

Many amateurs should be using an 11° or even 12°driver. As their skill level improves, they may graduate to a 10° or even a 9° loft on the club face. As you progress in your golf adventure, you will realize that you do not yet have the abilities to use certain types of equipment. Most of us should start with the easier to hit 'game improvement' type of clubs at the beginning which make it easier to launch the ball and get it up in the air.

As your skills increase, it will become clear to you that an equipment upgrade will force you to refine your swing for the next phase in your growth and progress. When does that happen? You will know when, but remember the results of a golf swing are 80% the skill of the golfer and about 20% the ball/equipment that he employs.

The fairway woods are to me easier versions of the driver in that the loft (or degrees of tilt of the club face away from the target) for the fairway woods is between 15° and about 21°. This greater loft of the club face is the major factor controlling how accurate a given club is for the amateur.

In the old days, the pros like Nicklaus, Hogen, or Tiger Woods, and many others hit 1-iron and 2-irons that the average amateur today would have very little hope of using effectively. In fact, today many sets of irons have a 4-iron or 5-iron as the most difficult to hit irons and the longer missing irons, typically a 3-iron or 4-iron have been totally replaced by the modern hybrid clubs.

Hybrids have taken their rightful place in everyone's golf bag and here is how I proved it to myself. When I replaced my 3-iron with a hybrid, I took both clubs to the back yard and got out my trusty pack of 7 wiffleballs. I set about hitting the balls toward a target and it didn't take long at all to convince myself that the hybrid with its' curved face and hollow body actually hit those wiffleballs about 10% further and the accuracy (in the tightness of the dispersion pattern) was also better.

Those results were difficult to argue with and after putting those hybrids into my bag, I have never had second thoughts.

The last group of clubs which are the shortest and heaviest in your bag are the wedges which you use for short range work around the green typically from about 120 yards in to very close to the green. We should think of these as our 'scoring' clubs and they really are the difference between those people that just show up and those who contend for the trophy.

There are also some specialized wedges called sand wedges typically 54° to about 58° in loft that many people use from the sand traps as well as gap or approach wedges usually in the 48° to 52° range used from a little further away from the green. In any case, these clubs are the real money makers and if I can practice with only one club leading up to that week's competition, for me that would be my 50° Gap wedge.

In my opinion, the strongest shot in golf competition is not that long initial drive that out-distances the other guys by 30 yards. The shot that will really demoralize your competitor is the wedge shot that you execute onto the green; the one that stops two and a half feet from the flagstick for an easy tap in with your putter. Once the other guys see that shot, they know you have already won that hole.

Become a strong wedge player and you will certainly have a good chance to see yourself in the final show-down later in the season. When you become that contender near seasons end, that is the excitement that this book is written to capture.

The other key part of our golfing equipment is the golf ball. I have already spoken about the benefit of the wiffleball for practice and club evaluation purposes. We should now turn our attention to real golf balls and how to pick one appropriate for your skill level.

Let's face it, there are a lot of balls available out there, but they are not all created equal and even more importantly not all are appropriate for amateurs. For those of us with low skill levels and slow swing speeds, a different style of ball is required to supply us with the most enjoyable results when we swing that club and strike that ball.

I offer a short story about some advice I had passed on to a Technical Director I once worked for. He was a very average golfer of moderate abilities and I heard him complaining that his ball was always ending up in the deep rough and rarely found the short grass in the fairway. One day in the hallway at work I said to him 'Hey, have you tried the straight flight Noodle ball that I have been using lately?' He said no and I explained that I had found I could play nine holes and almost never get into the rough. Several weeks later I ran into him and he said 'Thanks Rhandy, I tried that ball you mentioned and I played great with it'. He could not believe that he was now in the fairway.

Of course, there are many straight flight type balls out there. I have had personal success using the Bridgestone e6 and e7 as well as the Titleist DT Solo. My recent favorites have been the Callaway Hex Control and finally in 2018 the Callaway SuperHot55 was my ball of choice. Let me retrace my steps a little and explain the importance of the golf ball.

In my early days of golf, I would play any ball I happened to find or any that was given to me. Before my enlightenment, a ball was a ball. It was just a white target that my club head attempted to find. At some point in 2005, I realized that every time I hit a nice shot into a green, the ball landed on the green and just continued to roll until it reached the far side of the green and rolled off the back side.

As I picked up my golf ball after completing the hole, I thought 'maybe I need to try another brand of ball'. I started to read up on different ball designs and decided that the Titleist NXT sounded like a good change to me and it certainly was. In fact, I consistently played that ball for five years and it was the first ball that I broke a hundred with on a real golf course. My score that day in 2006 was a 47 on the front nine and a 47 on the back nine for a new best score of 94 strokes. Since that time, I have not hit a single one of those 'rocks' that used to roll off the back side of the green.

From that time forward, I realized the power of using a ball appropriate to my skill level. I also realized that by sticking to one ball, that element of the game did not become an added variable as I studied other areas of my game. For those people who switch balls every time they turn around, they have no idea if they should blame a problem on the club, their swing, or the 'new' golf ball they just found in the deep rough.

How do people measure progress in their golf game? One indicator of how well I am playing is the number of balls I lose during play. When I am playing really well, I may play for a stretch of three or four weeks without losing a ball. What this really means is that I am hitting fairways and greens and the rough is not being visited very often.

The other notable piece of golf equipment that most players use and rely upon is their golf glove. If you ever see me playing, you might notice that I don't wear a glove unless the snow is falling in October and then I am wearing two winter golf gloves to keep my hands from freezing.

The reason I don't wear a conventional glove is that I learned the game during the period when Fred Couples was number one in the world and I saw that he did not wear one at that point in time. I also noticed that each time I tried to wear a glove, it seemed to work well when it was brand new. However, as it wore out, the gripping affinity of the glove for the club's grip began to diminish. Eventually, I felt like the glove was becoming slippery and a psychological nuisance to me.

The last piece of equipment I will speak of is the putter and that discussion will be contained in the Putting chapter of this book.

Chapter 7:   Record Keeping, Swing Keys Card, Yardage Card, and measuring progress

This chapter is much of the reason I am writing this book and it is also where you are offered some unique methods for controlling and understanding your personal progress in the game. I have found that if I consistently have 3x5 index cards available during practice and play, then I am able to take important notes about technical points like set up procedures, grip, club choices, alignment notes, impact points on the club face, etc.

These kinds of notes can actually supply benefits even years later. I know you are thinking 'oh yeah how can a few jotted down notes help me three years from now?' We have all heard the expression 'that's like catching lightning in a bottle'. For me, one of those 'lightning in a bottle' moments arrived at the driving range in September of 2010.

It was September 21st and I had made some minor modifications to my swing and I wanted to see if they held up at the range. What happened there that day was like a dream. No matter which club I pulled from the bag, the ball flew out there and landed within about 10 feet from my target. I'm not talking about just wedge shots. I mean all the clubs. The long irons, the short irons, the hybrids, even my driver was acting like a heat seeking missile.

That was magical, but what I did next was the really important part. I took out my pen and 3x5 index card and jotted down the details of my set up, my grip, special notes on new swing modifications and I did capture 'some lightning in a bottle' for later use. As I make further modifications to my swing, I use those important previously dated memo cards to expand my knowledge of my swing and my personal physiology.

That driving range card is shown here in Figure 1. and captures many of the vital points. As the years went on from this point, I continued to keep notes on improvements as they occurred and was able to produce optimum swing cards for both driving and for putting procedures.

Golf: Best Driving Range Results Ever
9-21-2010 (6 days after Firestone)

Goal: to correct bobbing of head downward during downswing.

Solution: i) keep eyes glued to ball to keep head steady.
ii) Play ball at bottom of Left Hand Only swing arc.

Result: I could point anywhere on the range and land the ball within 10 feet (Even with my 11° driver).

Details: Address ball with feet together & perpendicular to target line

Ball Position: 11° Driver = ½" left of Left Heel
3W & 3Hyb = in line with Left Heel
3 iron = 1" Right of Left Heel
Mid & Short Irons = 2" Right of Left Heel
Wedges = 3" Right of Left Heel

Figure 1. Catching 'Lightning in A Bottle'.

These Swing Key-Points cards are really a check list of points to consider before beginning play or practice. My typical Swing Key-Points card is shown in Figure 2. This is a great tool to keep us on track in our performance. It helps eliminate that feeling we might have after a round of golf, when we wonder "what happened?" A quick glance at our card, usually reveals immediately what key point we neglected in our swing.

Rhandy's Ultimate Swing (Based on impact position of body on 7-21-10) MARCH 2017

1) Stand to ball holding club in left hand only. Cinch club w/ left hand.
2) Lightly add right interlocking grip. Torso slight tilt with arched back.
3) Arms close to torso at address & during take away.
4) Feet: 60% of weight on balls of feet.
5) During take away create tension in calves & gluts.
6) Maintain straight left arm during 3/4 take away.
7) Turn toward the target in down swing right elbow sync. with torso.
8) Keep eyes locked on ball.
9) Swing through ball, keep left wrist flat & follow line.
10) Finish with full follow through & in balance.

Figure 2. Swing Key-Points card.

Once you begin to do this type of brief check-up, you will be amazed by the benefits of using these checklists. What I usually discover is that I gave little or no attention to point #5 on my card and I really paid the price. These cards are a great way to tune up your swing before you even touch a club.

Another important tool we need to make for ourselves is a yardage guide for our clubs. For me this is a card that lists all the clubs in my bag. Next to each club, I list the actual typical yardage that each club delivers. This is not a list of 'what I wish my clubs delivered', but instead is that real yardage number that the clubs deliver 80% of the time.

When we are honest with ourselves and use these real yardage numbers, the result will be that our shots will most often reach the green and not fall short. When we fall short of the green, we have often added an extra stroke to our score card and that is never a good thing. See Figure 3. for my Club Yardage card.

In addition, we should also compile some additional yardage numbers for what I call half shots. These are the results that I get when I take my small clubs only half way back into my backswing before pulling the trigger. For me a half shot means the club goes back until it is level with the ground and then I initiate the forward part of my swing.

I am then able to deliver a 50-yard shot with my pitching wedge or I can deliver a 60-yard shot with my 9-iron. Many people can only make a wild guess about these tough to dial in distances, because they never took any time to practice these half shots. Also determine for yourself what your half-shot yardages are for your 8-iton, 9-iron, Pitching Wedge, Gap Wedge, and Sand wedge. These difficult half-shots are like money in the bank when you produce them at the right time.

My Actual Club Yardages

1 Wood	= 230	Pitching Wedge	= 90
3 Wood	= 190	Gap Wedge	= 75
2 Hybrid	= 165	Sand Wedge	= 60
3 Hybrid	= 155		
4 iron	= 150		
5 iron	= 140		
6 iron	= 130		
7 iron	= 120		
8 iron	= 110		
9 iron	= 100		

Figure 3. Actual Club-Yardages card.

The concept of measuring progress is to me also about keeping track of our progress. Is our handicap inching downward to a lower number where we would like to be? Or is our handicap creeping upward as we neglect our game and the things required for improvements in our performance.

Once you begin to assemble and use these tools, you will indeed find you are in control of your own destiny. You will find that you now have the tools to know what works for you and much of the frustration and the 'trying-mode' will disappear from your pursuit of golf. In the next chapter we turn our attention to putting and will use some similar techniques to take control of that half of our game.

Chapter 8: Putting is………… Half the Game

For those of you who don't see much excitement in this portion of the game, I can only say "Get over it". Putting usually represents half the strokes you will record on your scorecard. Also, guess what. That eight-inch tap in putt from your failed birdie attempt, counts exactly the same amount of damage on your scorecard as that 280-yard best drive you ever had! That's right, they both count one stroke each. We can't get away from this area of the game and should really embrace putting as a way to relieve pressure created by other areas of our game that might be struggling a bit on any given day.

I have always been a fairly good putter and will share the things that have been helpful for me. One of the ways I prepare for the golf season during the winter months in the north is to watch golf on television and set up my tape measure on the rug in front of my television and then I practice putting balls to a three-inch wide target or better yet at a golf ball sitting across the room. What I like to do is drop a ball six feet from the target, then another nine feet from the target and finally one at twelve feet from the target.

Then what I like to do is figure out what kind of takeaway distance does each of these putts require. What this does is to give us a good guess about what a ten-foot putt might feel like. As conditions appear on the golf course, I often think to myself, "this uphill putt is only six feet, but needs to be struck like a nine-foot putt due to that extra slope upward".

Back in my living room, I might find that a six-inch takeaway might produce a six-foot putt. An eight-inch takeaway might produce a nine-foot putt. A ten-inch takeaway might get us to the twelve-foot putt we are attempting. In any case, this represents some good mental conditioning that can create good putting performance, once we reach the real golf course.

Another important thing I have found in the living room is that I can also improve the aiming of the putt and for me this relies heavily on the type of putter I prefer. I have preferred the mallet style and more specifically, I use one of the Taylor Made Spyder putters because it has a very long alignment line etched into its' top surface. For me this line makes it very easy for me to know where my putter face is pointed.

In fact, what I have found is that as I begin to line up this line with the target, I do something a little counter intuitive. As my first step, I intentionally make sure this line is pointing several degrees right of my target line. Then with one or two slight adjustments toward the left, I bring it back to my target line and when I am fully there, I complete the putt.

This can work great for a five-foot putt or a twenty-foot putt. The accuracy of this technique can be very impressive. In my living room, I can use this method and stack up golf balls against my small target one after another from twelve feet away. See Figure 4 for a picture of my actual Putting Keys card that I developed that winter before the 2014 golf season.

In the equipment section we did not talk about putters and for many people this is a very personal kind if choice. I have already explained my preference for mallets with their long alignment lines. Each of you need to try out a bunch of putters at a golf show or at your local golf shop to see which one works best for you. It may not be the highest priced one, but when you find your best match you will know. When that special putter shows up, the putts will begin to drop with less effort and your confidence will soar. You will suddenly feel like the putter is almost like a customized extension of your arms.

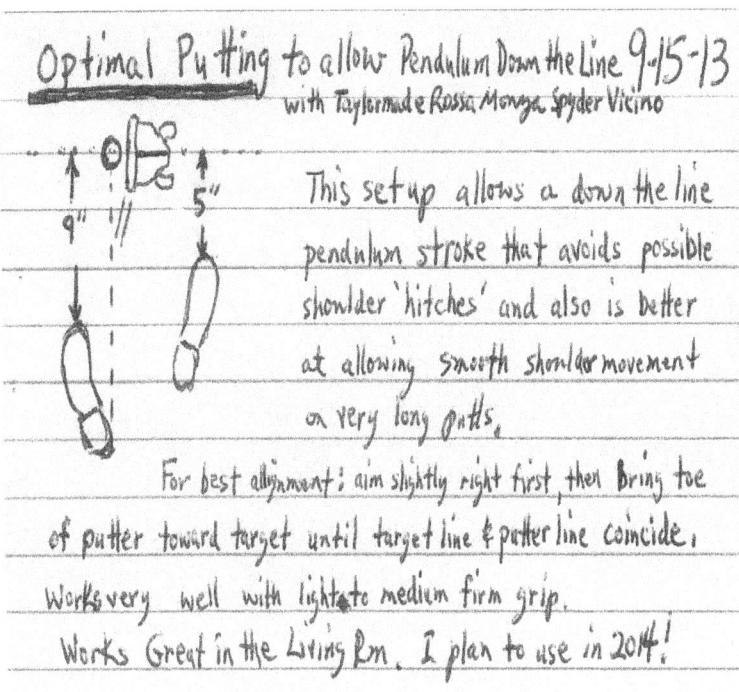

Figure 4. Putting-Keys card

Once you find that special 'friend', your putter will probably be with you for a very extended time. Certainly, it will stick around for years and possibly even for decades. I guess names like Corey Paven and Ben Crenshaw both great masters of the 'flat stick', come to mind as men who used the same putter for decades. Another great player in that regard is certainly Jack Nicklaus, who appears to still be successfully using that same putter immortalized during his heyday.

My final recommendation on putting is that you get the right putter and practice with it until you become proficient. If you find you are still struggling, get a lesson from a local golf professional or buy a good book on putting by someone like Dave Stockton. Remember that putting will always be half the game, so give it the attention it deserves.

Chapter 9:   Physical Conditioning & Mental Preparedness

This topic relating to physical conditioning kind of was off my personal radar until about the time Tiger Woods was dominating the tour and began to show up at the course with a much more physical presence. I too began to realize that having a little more upper body strength could directly translate to much more club control at the top and bottom of my golf swing.

Once I consciously began to work on a little strength training, I could tell that my play improved and I was able to play just as well during the back-nine as I was during the initial front-nine. In years past, my back-nine scores were always invariably slightly higher numbers. I always attributed that to getting tired and running low on 'steam'.

The physical part of the game is certainly important and even though I am getting into the higher age brackets, I stubbornly continue to be a walker on the course whenever that is possible. To me this does more than offer exercise. It also offers a couple of advantages that the riders don't get.

For me, walking allows my spine to continue to stay in alignment, because I am not slouched over on those terrible seat cushions. Secondly, as I walk down the fairway to my next shot, I am able to calmly evaluate the previous shot as well as the shot that is coming up shortly. For me this is very emotionally empowering and my muscles are fully stretched and ready to perform when I reach my ball.

The mental preparation for play is a pretty important as well and golf is certainly just as much mental as it is physical. We are apt to arrive at the course in a variety of mental conditions. For many of us, we just left work an hour ago and often are carrying a lot of very negative baggage with us. Don't drive to the course listening to a News station that is really just the echo chamber for some political party. Leave that hate and other negative energy along the roadside somewhere before you get close to the course. You should walk onto the course with a relaxed, confident attitude. Turn off your phone and enjoy this walk in the park.

A short word about determination or if you will 'grit'. If you are serious about becoming a real contender this year, then you need to toughen up. Realize that the difference between first place and second place comes down to that grit or will-to-win element that the victor arrives with. Remember, if you forgot to bring any of your own grit, your competition will show you his.

Grit does not mean gamesmanship, but it does mean you are focused on the business at hand and are in the awareness zone. You are not there to laugh at his nervous jokes. You are there to deliver the full measure of what you have proven to yourself at the range and have shown to others in previous victories.

If a bad shot happens, you will shake it off, analyze what happened, make the needed adjustment, and execute your next shot in the proper manner. You will remain a gentleman, but one who is focused on his game.

When you first arrive at the course, you should arrive with confidence because you have been documenting progress at the range and in your previous competitions. You have a card in your pocket that tells all you the real yardages for your clubs. You have another card in your wallet that spells out the Ten Key-Elements of Your Ideal Swing. To put it simply, you have arrived fully prepared and confident that you will make every shot count. Now go out there and have a good time and a great round of golf with your buddies.

Chapter 10:   The Game of Games, Honor of the Game, the Mystique of Golf

To me golf is a wonderful game and actually much more than a game. I call it the 'Game of Games', because it is so revealing in the lessons taught and the responses of those being taught. No other game can be viewed from so many different viewpoints and can challenge an individual for their entire lifetime.

I always ask, "What game is there, that a 70 year old man in average health can beat an athletic young man of 20 years of age?" In my mind, golf is the natural answer. Golf is a great equalizer. In many regards it is able to cut across all demographics and income classes. When we play, we all become equals as we struggle and persevere. We feel the same anguish and the same exhilaration whether we have hit that shot or it was struck by our direct competitor. We acquire a sense of empathy for others and develop what might be described as a conscience.

We learn the concept of fair play without having to resort to treachery or falsehoods of any kind. On the golf course we are taught the concept of honor and actually call the penalties on ourselves. What an incredible business model.

To many people outside this game, the concept of calling a penalty on yourself is very baffling. They think, "why would anyone do that to themselves?" To self-centered narcissistic personalities, the world is all about exploiting the weak and achieving our own personal desires by any means available. We live in a time when the people that used to be pillars of admiration and respect are now routinely marched off to prison for being liars, thieves, and con men on the grandest scale imaginable.

I see this game as offering the average person a chance to walk on a little higher spiritual plane, if only for a few hours each week. To show others what a sense of fair play and moral behavior is apt to look like. For many of us, this feels like a brotherhood of like-minded souls. We feel like Don Quixote tilting at windmills in a game we know can never be totally mastered by these mere mortals.

As I think back to that day in 1990, at my first trip to the driving range with my golf mentor Bernie, I had no inkling what lay ahead. I placed that first ball on the tee, swung the club back and through and the strike felt pure and true. I can still hear Bernie's words with an encouraging tone in his voice "Look at that Rhandy, you are a …………..natural."

Submitted to you in the hopes that you too can appreciate all the wonder of golf as much as I do.

Rhandy X. Jedermann 2019

www.ingramcontent.com/pod-product-compliance
Lightning Source LLC
Chambersburg PA
CBHW031437040426
42444CB00006B/847